T0196217

HEALTHCARE DECIPHERED

EXPOSED AND UNCENSORED

THE REAL GUIDE TO LOWERING COSTS AND AVOIDING DENIALS

RACHEL BORYACHINSKIY

HEALTHCARE DECIPHERED

Exposed and Uncensored

Rachel Boryachinskiy

authorHOUSE®

AuthorHouse™
1663 Liberty Drive
Bloomington, IN 47403
www.authorhouse.com
Phone: 1 (800) 839-8640

This book is a work of non-fiction. Unless otherwise noted, the author
and the publisher make no explicit guarantees as to the accuracy
of the information contained in this book and in some cases, names
of people and places have been altered to protect their privacy.

Published by AuthorHouse 02/21/2017

ISBN: 978-1-5246-6038-3 (sc)
ISBN: 978-1-5246-6036-9 (hc)
ISBN: 978-1-5246-6037-6 (e)

Library of Congress Control Number: 2017902375

Print information available on the last page.

This book is printed on acid-free paper.

Because of the dynamic nature of the Internet, any web addresses or
links contained in this book may have changed since publication and
may no longer be valid. The views expressed in this work are solely those
of the author and do not necessarily reflect the views of the publisher,
and the publisher hereby disclaims any responsibility for them.

This book was completely edited by Kelly Barkley Mane.

Visit our website at www.healthcaredeciphered.com

Contents

As a bonus, Lightning Facts are included at the end of each chapter.

Need to Know – This section is a quick summary of the major points listed in the chapter that help at a glance. These can also be used as a fast method to reference facts when you need a refresher later.

Take a Moment – These steps should be completed after each chapter, before moving to the next chapter. We've created a step by step handbook to ensure you are not overpaying on medical expenses. Following our simple process will ensure you are paying correctly. If you catch an issue, we also provide steps to get corrected. If at the conclusion of the handbook you still have questions send us an email, <u>customerservice@healthcaredeciphered.com</u>, for free!

Acknowledgements

This handbook is written for everyone, regardless of experience with healthcare. My goal is to inspire more engagement. We are wasting money on medical expenses without even realizing. Given the overall spending in healthcare, we cannot afford to be careless. I know from my own personal experience.

If you are reading this handbook, you are already getting more help. It is a step to help simplify a complex industry. Our goal is to provide tools to help you decipher healthcare. That's the foundation of our company. We take the headache out of healthcare!

Thank you to supporting our company and allowing us to help you. We are truly humbled by our clients and supporters.

A special thank you to the contributors, who helped write and/or edit this handbook. Without your influences, we would have never reached our goals. Cheers to a bright future.

A note from the Author

Healthcare is frustrating, complicated, and overall boring. This is the reason most are completely unengaged in their health insurance or any other administrative components of their care. However, much like the buying any item on the market today, if you do not do your research, you could be left paying thousands more than necessary.

This is the reason for the book. The goal is to enhance the healthcare experience by providing usable, relevant industry knowledge in a way that is easily understood. The only people engaged in healthcare, in most instances, are other healthcare professionals. I'd like to change this trend.

You have to take an active role to prevent overspending! The only way to own your experience is to have a degree in healthcare currently. This book prevents the need for higher education, breaking down the industry into a handbook for success. By applying a few steps, everyone can decrease the amount paid on everything from doctor visits to large hospital bills. In addition, we help provide undisclosed secrets about your health insurance company.

I spent years working for health insurance companies, aka health plans, in a variety of departments. My role was to ensure the health plan's operations ran seamlessly. I worked with every department, across multiple products yielding an extremely extensive knowledge of health plan mechanics. I know all the intrigue details, you cannot find anywhere on the internet. To be honest, most of the specifics mentioned in the book are not even taught at the graduate level. You have to be in the industry.

The best part is I'm telling you now. It's time to start really explaining how health plans work. We need to be able as familiar with healthcare bills, as we are with our everyday utility bills. I guarantee if the cable bill goes up, you notice. I know I do. This is the reason I'm creating a handbook and helping unlock the answers to all the questions you never knew to ask. How could you? You don't have a degree in healthcare, nor do you want one. Instead you can use my education and experience to navigate the industry like a pro.

Let's start by simplifying the complex healthcare jargon.

*If you are already familiar with this terminology, skip ahead to the introduction. We really dive right in.

Definitions

Health Plan – This is your health insurance company, often the big names you hear on tv. We are not allowed to mention, but it's the name on your insurance card. Hopefully, that is located in your wallet. Health plans have various products, which are the different types of service packages you can choice from. Most people are familiar with the gold, silver, and bronze product levels with ObamaCare.

Deductible – You have to meet this financial obligation every year. This is the established dollar amount the health plan sets that must be paid prior to the health plan paying for a portion of the health services. However, the deductible typically does not apply to routine or wellness visits.

Copay – This is the flat rate paid when you go for a healthcare appointment, which includes routine, preventative and wellness visits. This health plan pays the rest of the cost of services. If you are lucky, you have a lot of services in your insurance that are copays.

Cost sharing – is the portion of the overall bill the insurance plan splits with you. Most cost sharing plans have member responsibility around

10-30% of the total costs per service. The health insurance pays the remaining portion of the bill. Of course, this only happens after you meet your deductible for the year.

Coinsurance – This is the percentage of the total allowed after the deductible and copay have been applied to the bill. The health plan pays a portion of the remaining costs for the service and you pay the balance.

Out of Pocket Limit – This is the highest dollar amount you will pay in a given benefit year for health services. After the out-of-pocket maximum is reached the health plan will pay 100% for any remaining health services in the same benefit year.

Annual Benefit Limit – The annual benefit limit is the most the health plan will pay for you in a given year before you start paying 100% for the remaining health services in a given benefit year.

Pre-authorization – This is VERY IMPORTANT. Authorization for services must be obtained prior to any services being rendered for you. The authorization is a medical determination the health services are medically necessary and appropriate levels of care for you. If you or your doctor do not obtain, you will be left paying the entire bill.

Provider Network Participation – Your health plan determines the types of doctors, hospitals, etc. that are contracted to provide services to you, under your plan. Often referred to as 1 of the below:

1. PAR (Network Provider) – One of the options your health plan offers
2. Non-PAR (Non-Network Provider) – Not an option, unless you want to pay more out of your own pocket. There are only a few exceptions, which we discuss later.

Billing/Claims

Explanation of Reimbursement – The below components that Health plans use to explain how payment was applied to your service (claim).

Billed Amount – This is the total charges from the provider, which may not necessarily be the contracted amount negotiated between the prayer and the provider based on the contract. The billed amount is particularly important for providers who are not part of the network, who can bill you for services not paid by the health plan.

Allowed Amount – The allowed amount is the contracted amount the plan and the provider have agreed to for services. A participating provider agrees to take this amount as payment in full and cannot balance bill you for the difference. This is not the case for providers who are not part of the network as there is no negotiated amount for services with the health plan.

Member Responsibility – Your responsibility is a combination of the copay, deductible, coinsurance, and not covered amount per service. The payment is described on the Explanation of Benefits (EOB) or online portal

Adjustments – Changes the Health Plan made to your claim, which may positively or negatively impact you.

Appeals and Grievances – For the initial EOB, this section will describe the process to submit an appeal or grievance on your behalf, if you are unhappy with the way the health plan initially processed your claims. If you have asked the Health plan to re-evaluate your initial claim, this section will denote the results on the adjusted claim EOB.

Chapter 1 – Introduction

Why costs matter

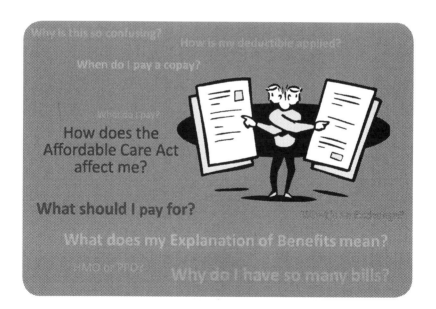

How does the Affordable Care Act affect me?

What should I pay for?

When do I pay a copay?

What does my Explanation of Benefits mean?

Why do I have so many bills?

Introduction

How much are you really spending on medical benefits? The average family of 4 in the U.S. spends over $25,000 a year on healthcare, which is over 50% of the average income of $54,000 per family as reported by the U.S. Census in 2015. Healthcare after the ObamaCare reform continues to rise by double digits each year overall. Historically, the financial impact felt by individuals was minimal as doctors absorbed the costs. These days, it is a little different.

Physicians and other types of providers are no longer making enough money to write-off the costs. It was easier to absorb costs, since the insurance payments to providers covered all most all service costs. Insurance companies have had to reduce costs in every area affecting the business, this includes payments to providers. Health plan types changed too. Members (You) have high deductible plans that are more of a financial burden on families. This is important as you are paying more and more for healthcare services.

In 2001, the average per family spent on healthcare was roughly $8,000, but in 2017 it is projected to increase to over $26,000. For a family of 4, this is an increase of 300% (Milliman, 2015). In comparison, inflation only increased 2% per year or 32% from 2001 to present. This enormous increase is regardless of health plan. Whether you have employer-offered, independent, exchange, or Medicare, you are feeling the financial burn.

Historically, employers paid 65% or more of their associates' healthcare premiums. In order to incentive businesses, employers are no longer required to contribute a specific percentage to offer benefits to their employees. Due to increased medical expenses, more employees in the workforce are struggling. Historically, employer-based insurance plans were the best and most cost effective. This is no longer the case.

Today, employers are paying about 50% of healthcare premiums, leaving their employees to pay the remainder of the cost. This drastic change is particularly important, as the rising costs shifting to employees is a combination of factors. You are required to pay a higher percentage of your premiums, premiums are increasing annually, deductibles have tripled in the last few years, and your overall percent of the remainder of the bill (co-insurance) is higher. Benefits are moving away from flat dollar (copayments) amounts for services. Instead the cost is shared between the health plan and you. This is true despite the type of coverage. Why is this happening?

There are several factors affecting the costly increases. The major factor is profit margins are smaller and smaller.

Physicians and hospitals are not the only impacted organizations, as health plan profit margins are now regulated thanks to the passage of The Affordable Care Act. The Affordable Care Act states health plans are limited to 15% in profits and 85% of the revenue has to be used strictly for care management plans for their members (*you*) (thehill.com, 2013).

Health Plans are Alike

Most health plans have very similar structures. The core departments and functions are almost identical, because functionally it works. Health plans, much like other industries, are constantly evaluating processes and streamlining. The core is constant: customer service, clinical, operations, and analytics.

The similarity will be both to your benefit and misfortune. The benefit is a few simple rules can be easily utilized across multiple health plans. The bad news is that health plans have similar issues, related to benefits, claims, appeals, and business problems. Most even structure with implementing the constant legislative changes.

Why does this matter?

Despite the significant financial impacts, $1.5 billion of health care costs is due to claim errors each year. The astonishing part is that you pay over 25% of the costs of these errors each year. The remainder of the cost is paid by Medicaid, Medicare, employers, etc. Basically, we are sharing the cost. The more significant issue is it is difficult to truly track this problem. Health plans self-reported to Consumer Reports that in the last few years claims are processed with over 90% accuracy. However, this is really impossible to independently measure.

Health plans process claims based on their system guidelines, which change almost daily. In addition, if a physician, hospital, or other healthcare providers bill in error the claim is rejected or denied. From the health plan's perspective the rejection or denial was processed correctly. However, the claims in these situations contained errors. It is up to the physician to fix and re-submit. More often, the physician bills the patient directly. At this point, it is up to you to identify the source of the error. The clincher is the health plan sent you a letter denoting the error, but did you catch it? Likely, you didn't. On top of not catching the error, you just paid the bill from the physician too. Therefore, there is no incentive for the physician to send a corrected claim as the physician just got paid by you. It is estimated that 80% of claims contain errors, as reported by the Wall Street Journal.

Despite the commonality of billing errors, many people do not know how to spot a billing error on their claim. The Washington Post surveyed 11,000 people and only 5% (550) could identify an error. In comparison to the total U.S. population of 321,442,019, this means only 16,072,101 people really have any idea what medical billing errors resemble.

To put this in perspective, there are 12,219,330 people in the healthcare industry (KFF.org, 2016). Therefore, 80% of the people who can identify errors are within the healthcare field. This means that most Americans, in other industries, cannot recognize claim/bill issues. Despite the fact that the information is listed on your eligibility of benefit statements from the health plans.

Health care is a confusing industry, which principles are opposite traditional business rules. Traditional business rules state higher demand lead to more product purchases and a greater bottom line. However, in healthcare higher demand is a result of a mismanaged population with increasing medical needs. An effective treatment plan reduces increases in services and limits demands. The concentration in healthcare focuses on the health of the patient; therefore, operationally there is room for improvement.

Healthcare costs are increasing at more than 3 times the rate of inflation. In addition, medical debt is the leading cause of bankruptcy in the U.S. Furthermore, almost 40% of U.S. citizens have medical bills that are with collection agencies due to non-payment (The common wealth fund, 2011). The average medical debt is almost $2,000 per family (Consumer Financial Protection Bureau (CFPB), 2014). The best way to eliminate medical debt is to verify accuracies. It is estimated that 80% of claims/bills have errors, which in turn leads to billions being unnecessarily overpaid. Whether you have medical debt or not, stop overpaying. Overpayment is costing us thousands per family each year. It is time to get to a better healthcare state. Let's start with building a better team to investigate and resolve issues.

Lightning Facts

Need to Know Facts

At the end of each chapter is a summary of the major points. This is the foundation of your health plan resource. The combination of facts will allow you to obtain a better healthcare state, our goal. The cost of healthcare is significant and increasing. The only way to guarantee accuracy is to review everything. We provide a manageable guide to verify your costs with emphasize on how to correct any billing errors. Why is this important? Let's review.

1. The average family spends $25,000 a year on healthcare (including premiums, deductibles, co-insurance, and other out of pocket expenses)
2. Costs are increasing across the board for physicians and insurance companies. These costs are being largely paid for by you
3. Contributing to a large portion of the overall costs are errors
4. The majority of people do not know how to check their claim for accuracy
5. Health plans are similar, so one set of guidelines can be applied universally to get cost verification for you.

Take a Moment

Are you ready to get to a better healthcare state? Take a moment to add up the amount you, your family or business, have spent on healthcare in the last year. **Add it all up!**

Tweet with **#MedicalCostsAddeditup!** on our feed: ***@HCDeciphered***. For each tweet, you will get to ask our team of professionals a FREE question.

Chapter 2 – Healthcare State

These resources should be familiar

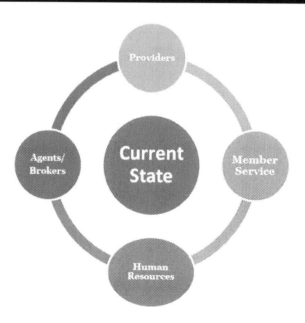

Current State of Healthcare

For the successful accomplishment of every task there is a team, healthcare is no different. Your current healthcare team has 4 or 5 positions, which are tasked with assisting you in obtaining healthcare services. Value should be the end result. Each portion of the team should be aiding you navigate healthcare without frustration or error. The problem is this rarely occurs. Despite the best intentions of most of your teammates on your health care team, health care is vast and changes almost daily making it difficult for even the best to keep up. Additionally, there is no requirement for people in these positions to have extensive health care knowledge.

Within your current state of healthcare, your team is generally made up of member services, sales brokers/agents, doctors, human resources. Each team member has positives and negatives, but does the team really support you? Let's dive into each aspect to find out.

Member Services

Have you ever called your insurance company? If so, you spoke to someone in the member services department. This department serves as the health insurance company's call center and your primary source of information for claims and benefits. Most call centers are based within the U.S. and often do not take calls after hours.

The call centers are designed to preserve relationships and provide information. However, usually the same representatives answer calls for each type of health plan that the insurance company offers For example, ABC Insurance Company offers 5 types of employee, Medicare, Medicaid, and ACA plans and only one member services center. This means that the member services center answers calls and fields questions for each plan. There is a burden on the member services staff to remember the nuances of each of the plans offered in order to provide accurate service to every caller.

Training to be a part of the member services department is provided by the health plan. However, there is no advanced degree requirement. The majority of representatives are required to have a high school diploma and a few years of call center experience. There are two distinct teams to help you and your doctor. Member service assists you, while provider services aids your doctor, hospital, and other providers. Healthcare companies do not require member service or provider service staff to have a healthcare background despite the vast array of information specific to care and coordination that is provided by the call center.

In addition, member service staff is not required to have knowledge of health plan operations. This is important, since most callers are asking for claim and benefit information. Member services, the team helping you, are provided with a general overview, but lack awareness on health plan basics. This is a problem.

This is very typical in the industry. While this may seem strange, the worst part is that the customer service ratings for healthcare are the lowest in the U.S. out of any other industry.

Call center ratings are measured based on the following criteria: average call duration, escalation rate, first call resolution rate, and time to resolution. The healthcare industry has the worst first call resolution rate by 14% lower than any other industry within the U.S (consumersunion, 2013). This means you are calling over and over again to obtain answers. The even scarier part is who knows which the correct response is. For example, you received a referral from your primary doctor for a specialist. You call member services to learn your options for a specialist, who participates with your health plan. If you are given inaccurate information by member services, you could be left paying the bill. Doctors have the same problem with provider services, often resulting in leading their patients in the wrong direction. Most mistakes are costly, resulting in callers being left guessing.

Member service staff can easily tell you any information that is already available on your insurance company's website or patient portal. This information includes effective date of service, level of benefits, if a claim has been processed, and anything that the health plan has done administratively.

Member services staff cannot help with the details. For example, if a claim processed with a denial. Member services can only regurgitate the information already listed on your eligibility of benefit statement, aka the letter from the insurance company that you throw out. In chapter 1, we mentioned this information is often not read by the average person. However, they cannot tell you really what the denial means. There are particular items that Member Services commonly end in mistakes.

For example, denials related to out of network provider. More often, these denials are related to processing issues by the health plan. For example, each time a claim is received from a doctor for your services, there is information that must match the health plan's system to electronically pay at participating rates. If for some reason, the health plan's system is not setup correctly, the claim will deny as out of network provider as a default. Providers struggle with these issues daily!

Another example is denials for no authorization. This is the pre-approval you received for services, generally before a surgery. The claim's date of service and service code, billed to the health plan for you by your doctor, has to match exactly to the information entered in the system for the authorization. If there is even a slight difference, again the claim will deny as no authorization. However, this does not mean you did not have an authorization. Just the health plan's system did not match to it electronically.

If either of these errors occurs, the member service staff can only tell you what the denial was, not how to fix it. We can help though! We discuss how to get errors fixed in a later chapter.

The highest chances of inaccuracies happen when determining if services needed by the patient require prior authorization, assisting a patient find an in-network provider, and understanding which specific services are covered by the insurance plan. What's the most common reason behind the high chance of inaccuracies? These items change regularly and are different dependent upon which plan a patient has. This makes it difficult for member services staff to stay up to date with the most current aspects of each health insurance member's plan. As such, there are no guarantees that the member services staff member you speak with is providing you, the client, with the right information.

Worried about what to do when you call member services with your questions? The best way to ensure you receive the right information is to keep a paper trail. All of the calls made to the member services department are recorded and monitored, both for training and quality assurance purposes. However, you have to call to yield the benefits later. Even if you think calling will be a waste of your time or frustrating. If the insurance company provided inaccurate information, they are liable for the mistake. You are not at fault financially, however, you have to be willing to track the information provided to you. The best way to keep track of the information is to create a paper trail in your documents. Take down the call number, date and time for your records, just in case you need to call back with a complaint.

Sales Broker and Agents

Another member of your healthcare team is your sales broker or agent, who can be affiliated or employed by the health plan. Agents and brokers help you obtain health insurance. If you do not have employer-based insurance, agents and brokers are your only source to get health insurance. Each agent is supposed to present the best possible health plan options for you. If there is a better option that is available, whether or not the agent sells this plan, the agent should make you aware of this option.

Hopefully, this is truly the case. If not, there are additional options available where you can buy insurance online or mail in the paperwork yourself. For these options, you need knowledge of benefits to ensure you are selecting the right plan. If the wrong health plan is selected, you could be left paying thousands more than necessary. Healthcare bills are the number one source of bankruptcy in the U.S. More information can be found at our blog, www.healthcaredeciphered.com, which can help if this becomes an issue for you. It may also be the subject of our next book in the series.

Agents and brokers are certified with a Life and Health Producer license by state in which they sell insurance. Each agent or broker has a license number and must adhere to a strict set of guidelines and principles as outlined by each state. If the agent or broker does anything that seems odd or is a violation, you can report the broker to the applicable state's insurance commission.

For example, if an agent or broker collects money from you, but you never receive a health plan, this is a violation. Common mistakes by broker are overpromising, not helping insurers pick the best plan, filling the application incorrectly, and more.

Brokers and agents are required to complete 40 hours of training, then take a test for their license. While this may seem like adequate training, it only covers an overview of the options available. Again, the details of each plan must be taught by the corresponding health plan. In addition, agents and brokers are not required to have healthcare backgrounds. While this may be adequate to help guide individuals in obtaining coverage, it does not necessarily mean that agents are able to serve as a well-rounded source of health plan knowledge.

Agents and brokers will refer you to the member services department for most questions. Some will try to help resolve an issue you might have, but it often takes significant time and resources ending in little success. Maintaining relationships is key to an agent's or broker's success. Unfortunately, their limitation is your frustration when trying to resolve any issue that arises with your insurance.

The other limitation is an issue of quality. Agents and brokers are similar to financial advisors, meaning personalities and skillsets vary greatly. Finding a good agent or broker is fundamental to obtaining a valuable health plan.

So what should you look for when choosing a health care agent? It is always best to select someone who can speak to a wide variety of plans, rather than one or two options. In addition, look for an agent or broker who has at least a few years of experience as healthcare has changed rapidly in the last 5 years and you want an agent who is familiar with the changes. An agent or broker who is well versed will provide the positive and negatives of each plan in simple understandable terms. If you are starting to get confused, move on to the next agent or broker. Enrolling in a plan that confuses you is not worth the risk, as most plans require a 12 month commitment and there are only certain times of year that you are eligible to enroll or change your plan. Finding a qualified agent or broker will lessen the likelihood that of making a wrong decision and being stuck with coverage with which you are unhappy. You can only change your insurance once a year, so you need to ensure it's the right fit.

Human Resources

If you have insurance offered through your employer, your primary contact is your Human Resources department. Human Resources (HR) helps set up your benefits, including health insurance. While HR works with an agency or health plan to provide benefits for their associates, often times HR does not manage the plan. Basically, the health plan still controls all aspects of the process, including benefits offered, setup, covered items, and claims processing.

If you are with a large organization, your company may own these rights. Meaning the company determines what benefits will be offered and covered. The only aspect in this situation the health insurance company manages is processing the claims and the provider network. If you are employed by a large organization, possibly National, likely your own human resources department selects what benefits to cover each year. This has nothing to do with your insurance company..... surprise!

If you want to find out who determines your benefits, you should reach out to your HR department. If the company determines the benefits, you may be able to ask them to cover certain items. In addition, the company has a better ability to resolve issues, as they are the decision maker.

The benefit of having an HR department is you have an issue, they should help. Now there are still limitations.

Most HR departments do not have a health plan operations expert in-house. This can be problematic for a few reasons. HR departments partner with Agents or Brokers to setup benefits for their employees. Without a health plan background, HR is at the mercy of the agent or broker; therefore this may not be advantageous. There are very few companies that survey their associates about healthcare, meaning most companies are making an assumption on the important aspects of a plan for you. This assumption may be cost effective for the employer, as high deductible plans are in demand at the moment. High deductible plans are not beneficial to you. High deductible plans require you to pay a fee before the health plan will start sharing the cost with you. There are deductibles up to $10,000 or more for families. Deductibles have to be met each year, leaving you will a significant financial out of pocket burden if you are using services.

Employer-provided healthcare plans are the main culprit for underinsured plans. Meaning employees do not have the right type of benefits for their healthcare needs, which in turn leads to high out-of-pocket costs. If you are underinsured, you are paying all-in (premiums, deductibles, and all other costs associated with healthcare) over 8% of your income. Employer benefits may not be the best option for you. Realizing the severity of underinsured employer-provided healthcare, the government has started to penalize companies who provide subpar benefits to their employees.

The caveat is whether you will qualify for another type of insurance, given financial and health status. If you have employer insurance, whether affordable or not, means you cannot qualify for another type of health plan. For people that have health issues, ObamaCare plans allow you to enroll. However, if you are offered insurance through your employer, you are not allowed to enroll. The kicker, if you have health issues likely you won't qualify for a private plan. Therefore, you are left with the unaffordable employer-insurance.

Furthermore, if something happens to you that results in your needing assistance with your plan, HR is given a resource at the health plan to contact for claims and benefit issues. The resource is usually within member or provider services.

HR cannot personally resolve the issue with the healthcare plan. The healthcare plan must correct the benefit or claim issue. However, depending on the "pull" of the HR department this may happen more quickly for some companies. You may be caught in the middle. If HR cannot resolve, you will be referred back to the member services department. This will only result in further time and frustration as nothing will have been solved. You will be back to square one.

HR wants to help, but a healthcare background is not a requirement for the position in HR. Companies with luck have a resource internally who can navigate or has knowledge of health plan operations. The problem is this is really difficult to find and may not necessarily be the top skill needed for the job. Therefore, you may be on your own.

All of the above players have little education related to health care, but are the core part of your team. I'm sure you are wondering how your doctor helps. Let's continue.

Doctors and Office Staff

There is one group on your healthcare team for which education is required and periodic training is encouraged. I'm speaking of course about your doctor. Your doctor, especially your primary care provider, is your first source for care. However, they dislike insurance companies as much as you do. The truth is health insurance is not part of the curriculum in medical school. Contrary to popular belief, there is no Healthcare 101 course. Navigating the healthcare system as a provider is a skill that is learned on the job or is handled by one of the office staff.

Often times, physicians have similar issues to you with insurance companies. The reason being, physicians are trying to get claims paid for the same visit and service that you are. It is advantageous to physicians to bill and follow protocols from the insurance company. If the physician doesn't bill appropriately, they have to submit corrected claims or an appeal. This means their payment is delayed or they may not get paid for services rendered.

The reason physicians have difficulty submitting claims are each insurance company has unique medical policies. Despite commonalities in departments and structure each health plan sets its own rules and guidelines. The physicians usually have different contracts with each insurance, meaning the services allowed, payment rate, and criteria for approval vary. Doctors have to balance their time with caring for patients and keeping a float administratively with health insurance companies. If the doctor is lucky, office staff help. However, to remain current doctors have to attend annual trainings from each health plan. As the rules and guidelines, change at least annually, if not more often.

Office staff generally handles the submission of claims. It is extremely challenging to have separate guidelines and programs. If claims cannot be submitted electronically, the alternative is to fax or mail the claims. However, there is no guarantee claims will be successfully submit to the insurance company, no matter the submission type.

There are training programs available to learn medical billing and coding, and many medical offices employ staff with such training. However, while the training can provide a foundation, there is no way for it to account for the ever changing landscape of healthcare insurance plans. The staff in charge of processing claims will still need to be in constant contact with the insurance company. Each time an approval for services is needed or it is necessary to check someone's benefits, office staff must call the insurance company. There is risk in receiving and interpreting information in appropriately, which leads to errors.

While physicians and office staff want to assist with administrative issues, often they're experiencing the same issues you face. It really takes a team to be able to navigate the various insurance guidelines. If the office staff do not follow all protocols sometimes the denial you receive is their fault. This is unintentional, but still ends in frustration for you.

Team Recap

Your current team tries to assist in their specific areas; sales, customer service, benefits, and care. However, the team does not provide a complete depth of knowledge necessary to fully aid you. The overwhelming gap in the healthcare industry is the administrative part. There are a few resources that provide assistance with benefits and claim issues, targeting the true costs and appropriateness.

Each visit to the doctor could end in overpayment, denial of benefits, or other unfortunate errors. Doctors and office staff try to avoid mistakes, but it is nearly impossible given the myriad rules and regulations from each health plan. Member services staff try to answer your questions; however, many are equipped with limited health plan operation experience. Your HR is on your side with a contact at the health plan. Depending on their level of involvement, results for you could be quick or nonexistent. Sales agents and brokers are eager to setup your benefits and get you started using the health plan. Once you start using your benefits, they take a back seat, leaving you to find alternatives to assist you.

Lightning Facts

Need to Know Facts

The team mentioned above should be familiar to you. If not, please take some time to evaluate how you can familiarize yourself with these key players. It is essential to be knowledgeable regarding resources available to you at each step of your healthcare journey.

1. The Member services department is your primary source for health benefit, network, and claim questions.
2. Member services is a call center and many staff likely do not have a healthcare degree.

3. Sales agents and brokers setup your individual health coverage. Most Sales agents and brokers possess only a cursory understanding of the intricacies of each health care option. Once your healthcare active, the sales agents and brokers take a backseat and the member services department is responsible for helping with any additional questions.

4. Human Resources is the best option for enrollment, problem resolution, and any other questions you may have with your employer-based insurance. However, the Human Resources department often does not have a background in health plan operations.

5. Doctors struggle with many of the same issues that you as the insured face. There are too many different health plans and products to easily master the process and requirement for each.

Take a Moment

Have you talked to any of these departments? If so, did you write down what information was given to you verbally or in writing? If not, start. This will play an important part of obtaining resolution successfully.

Chapter 3 – The "Power" Team

Let's add a few resources to the team

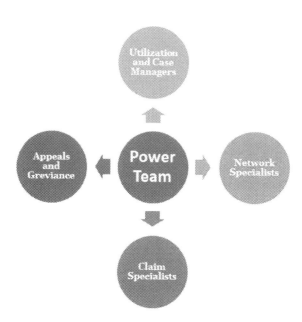

The "Power" Team

In chapter 2, we discussed the front-line team: customer service, brokers and agents, human resources, and your doctor. We highlighted the strengths of the front-line team and noted their areas of improvement. In this chapter, we go deeper and get a look at the team behind the front-line team. We've started with people who have basic health plan information, but the below are truly the experts. They are the additional departments within your health plan that are available to help you. Accessing these departments is a matter of knowing the right key words to ask.

Health plans are managed care organizations—they are businesses. Therefore, the health plan's goals are to reduce the cost of providing benefits, while increasing satisfaction in healthcare services. Health care plans want to be as effective as possible in the most cost-efficient manner.

Utilization and Case Managers

Most health plans have utilization management and case management departments. These departments are filled with nurses, Medical Directors, and other clinical staff. These departments monitor your health status to ensure services are appropriate, conditions improve, ensure checkups are completed, and your health is properly managed. The health plan manages your health to keep costs low. As you learned in Chapter 2, the Member Services department can provide basic details on your benefits, but if you have specific questions pertaining to a particular service or referral from your doctor, ask to speak with someone from the utilization or case management department.

If you require a service, such as a surgery or home health visit, the utilization management team reviews the doctor's documentation to ensure the need is appropriate and meets the health plan's criteria for approval. If the documentation is not specific or does not meet the health plan's certain criteria, the health plan will reject the request. If the doctor's documentation meets the required criteria, the health plan will approve the service for you. This is the prior authorization process.

Any time your health plan issues an approval or denial, you must be notified in writing of their decision. In addition, you must be allowed to contest their decision. You and your physician both have this right. If you receive a denial and would like more information the utilization and case management departments can provide the detailed rationale as to why. Furthermore, the staff in these departments can inform you if the denial can be prevented and if and how the decision can be overturned.

If you have had several medical concerns recently and would like assistance with your health coverage, ask your health plan to assign you a case manager. Case managers "work in conjunction with your medical services team to" help coordinate your care, ensuring you have all the essentials to get well. Case managers coordinate with your doctors, as well as, organize your care. Case managers having nursing degrees, who can advocate on your behalf with the health plan. The health plan pays case managers to manage your health. It is in the health plan's best interest to help you get better. Healthier members have fewer costs, which in turn means that the health plan saves money.

Now there may still be a few obstacles during this process, as the case managers are only able to suggest services that the health plan covers. However, if you require any additional service that is not typically covered having case managers will increase the likelihood the health plan approves under special circumstances. Remember that case managers work with your physicians as well. In a case manager, you have a patient advocate, who is bundled into your health plan at no additional cost.

If you are dealing with chronic healthcare issues make sure to ask to be assigned a case manager, instead of only speaking with the member services department.

Network Specialists

Member services staff can look up in the provider directory to tell the providers in-network vs out-of-network (participating vs non-participating). However, this is literally the same information that can be accessed by you directly from the health plan's website. If you need a specialty provider, the information is not easily available on the web or by contacting member services. Network Specialists have extensive knowledge of the health plan's network, as they built it.

Accessing the provider directory online can be frustrating. There may be multiple options, some better than others. In addition, providers are listed in different ways.

First, physicians can be listed by the overall group name of the practice, individually, or by hospital affiliation. If the physician's office is located within the hospital, they may not be noted in the provider directory search at all. To find these physicians, you may have to go to the hospitals website or search the services offered by the hospital. Physicians are added into provider directories based on the contracting and credentialing process. This is a very detailed analysis.

Second, if a physician has a subspecialty or offers a specific service then only the primary service or general category is denoted in the provider directory. For example, an orthopedic surgeon could specialize in knee and hip repairs. However, in the provider directory only orthopedic surgery would be listed. Also, durable medical equipment companies are notorious for offering different services. There is a wide variety of types and services. A durable medical equipment company who only provides wheel chairs as opposed to another company, who sells orthotics, is still categorized as durable medical equipment.

This is the reason sometimes it is difficult to locate a provider by calling member services or searching in the provider directory. A network specialist can provide detailed specifics on providers for your health plan. This way you get the right answer the first time.

Network specialists, also known as provider relations, and/or contracting analyst depending on the health plan, can help navigate your options within the health plan. If you do not receive adequate information from member services, ask to be transferred to a representative from the network specialists department for further assistance. Insist the member service representative follow-up with the Network team, who can provide an exact recommendation. Usually this is a time-intensive process but may be inherently important to you. Speaking with a representative from the network specialist department will help ensure that you receive accurate assistance. As opposed to only talking with the member services department, when you speak with a member from the network specialists department you are speaking with someone who has a background in healthcare. Thus, the information you receive is likely to be more in depth and comprehensive.

If there are no participating doctors that meet the criteria you need, the network specialist can help you get an authorization to go to a non-participating doctor. Why is this important? If you have approval from the plan to go to the non-participating doctor, the plan will pay the higher benefit level for you. Basically, you have less out of pocket costs. The caveat is you have to have the authorization before you go to services. The network specialist can help with this whole process, which makes it much easier.

Claim Specialists

The claim specialists process claims according to the rules and guidelines of the health plan. They also have intricate knowledge of how each service is paid. The claims specialists can help you get claims fixed and therefore, speaking with someone in this department is difficult. However, you can ask your member service staff to send your question directly to a claim specialist. Basically, bypassing member services, getting you right to the expert.

If a claim comes in from the doctor with the wrong diagnosis or an invalid code, it is up to the doctor to rebill the insurance company while you wait in the wind for updates. Often it is a simple fix to correct errors. The difficult part is obtaining the right information from the right department to fix the problem.

Often there is no number listed on your claim or the health plan's website that leads directly to the claims department, so you have to know what to ask for in order to get to the correct department. The member services team can ask the claims services department to review and provide feedback on your questions. If you are calling about claims dispute ask the representative from the member services department to send to the claims specialist for review and call you back in a few days. Remember in chapter 2, we discussed documentation. This is a very important process to track. If you do not obtain resolution, we will use this documentation in chapter 6 to escalate.

However, there is a more direct way to contact the claims specialists department. Login to your health plan's website and search for a "contact us" section. Many health plans now offer a live chat option with the ability to choose the department with whom you'd like to speak. Going online will help connect you with the claims team a lot easier and faster than calling and going through the member services department. This process is usually a lot easier and faster than phoning into member services.

There are two benefits to asking a claims specialist. Having the right information ensures you can easily verify everything is correct. If the answer seems complexing or confusing, likely it is wrong. Here is why.

If the medical provider billed erroneously, the claims specialist will provide detailed information on how to correct the bill. Armed with this knowledge, you can call your doctor's office to have them resubmit the claim. Furthermore, this will prevent you from being balance billed by the doctor when it is their error. This is often not intentional, but it is always better to verify.

The second benefit to having a claims specialist review your claims is that often times if the health plan is at fault, the health plan will re-process your claim without any additional documentation. This is called a reconsideration request, which can be initiated by the member services department. We discuss the reconsideration process in depth in chapter 6. For now, you just need to know it is an option. The member services department is responsible for submitting and tracking reconsideration requests. The process generally takes 10 business days to complete, ending in less work for you. Plus, the member services department has to follow-up with you directly on the result from submitting the reconsideration and you did not have to do any additional work.

Appeals and Grievances (Complaints)

Now there is another department that you should already be aware of, if not, you are missing out on an opportunity to obtain better resolutions, get back overpayments, and utilize your legislative authority. The appeals and grievances department, otherwise known as the complaints department, is your primary source for problem resolution. The Appeals and grievances department review service claims for things included but not limited to: medical necessity, network status, member complaints for care or service.

In order to have the best possible outcome when submitting an appeal it's important to know the following things. All communication with the department must be in writing. In addition, most plans only offer one opportunity to appeal with strict requirements of criteria to include. The rules and requirements for what must be included when appealing a decision are written in fine print at the bottom of your eligibility of benefit (EOB) statement.

The appeals and grievance teams will also accept and review service or care issues that developed while trying to utilize your benefits. This could be anything from scheduling to a surgical error. Health plans are required to track and investigate any complaints from their members. If the issues are valid, steps are taken to prevent them from occurring again in the future.

The other benefit of the appeals and grievance department is that the team has nursing backgrounds. This is important because if a claim was denied by the claims department, the appeals and grievance department can overturn the denial based on medical necessity. Appeals and grievances can request claims be reprocessed as well. This is part of their 30-90 day turnaround. While this may take a longer time period, than other options, the results are usually the most beneficial to you.

Power Team Recap

Having a deeper knowledge of how your health plan operates not only increases your knowledge into the process of your health plan but also increases your ability to access effective and efficient assistance to meet your needs. Armed with this information you are now able to go beyond your broker/agent and the member services department. In fact, you have four more options to utilize, when necessary.

The Utilization Management, Network Specialists, Claim Specialists, and Appeals & Grievances departments work for the health plan, but have access to intricate details that is absolutely beneficial to you. These departments are the team that can verify accuracy of claims, escalate, and resolve your issues.

Each area has their separate process and responsibilities, which must be followed to obtain additional information you are seeking. If you do not mind a little coordination, you will really be utilizing the full continuum of resources available to you from your health plan. The team is coming together, but there are some added details you should know.

Lightning Facts

Need to Know Facts

Now you have four additional resources to consider utilizing. The staff in these departments is considered the experts in their fields, driving a number of decisions by the health plan. In addition, all these departments have significant health care degrees, often at the graduate level equivalent.

1. Utilization and Case Managers are certified nurses and clinical staff with medical training. This area can help explain:

    Authorization requirements
    Approved health plan services
    Help manage your health

2. Network Specialists are the best resource to help identify doctors, facilities, and hospitals you can utilize. They can also help approve exceptions if there is a service gap.

3. Claim Specialists have intimate knowledge about how claims are processed. If anyone can help you verify accuracy, they certainly can review.

4. Appeals and Grievances are the last option to get resolution. We saved the best for last.

5. Make sure to get transferred appropriately to the right area.

6. Use these resources to get absolute clarity

Take a Moment

It is crucial to keep costs low. The only way to ensure accuracy is to follow-up regularly. Set aside time each month to review any documents you've received from your doctor or health plan. If something doesn't make sense, call. Taking an hour each month to review will really help to guarantee you do not over pay.

Chapter 4 – Where to Start

Take steps to verify costs easily

Where to Start

Now you know the people to contact, you are headed in the right direction. However, even with the experts at your fingers, there is still a problem that remains. Healthcare has its own language. To communicate effectively, you have to be well versed in the dialect. Literally, health plans, doctors, hospitals and every other provider all interconnect using codes. The codes are translated into policies, billing principles, diagnoses and procedures.

In order to work with the team on any questions, you have to translate the codes and their meanings into resolutions. Here are some health plan basics to start:

1. **<u>Always call to see if services are covered</u>**

    The Member Services department has a specific list of services by codes that are covered under your health plan. While your doctor might be familiar with some of the services, he or she will not know all of the services that your health plan covers. Just like you, your doctor calls a representative at the health plan to verify benefits.

    Now some information will be available in your member handbook. Services are listed generally by category. Likely, you have outpatient surgery benefits; however, is the colonoscopy through stoma: diagnostic, with or without collection of specimen(s) by brushing or washing covered? There is a chance the exact code is not on the health plan's approved list.

Therefore, the best advice is to ask the Member Services department before undergoing medical treatment. Remember, if the Member Services department provides the wrong information it is the health plan's fault. Therefore, if a claim is partially or fully denied, the health plan should re-process upholding their initial advice to you. This includes going to a non-participating provider accidentally, because you were told the provider was in network. Just remember to write down the date, time, reference number, whom you spoke with, and exactly what you were told. Member service calls are all recorded, so the health plan can refer back to the exact call to verify your claim. As long as you call to verify before you proceed with treatment, you have options. If you don't, you could be left with a costly mistake. Unsure of what to specifically ask when you call the member services department? Check out the "Need to Know Facts" at the end of the chapter for some sample questions.

2. **<u>Don't assume your doctor knows</u>**

Doctors want to do the very best for every patient every day. They receive years of training and continued education each year to assist you in staying healthy. You trust your doctor to help.

The issue is not with your doctor, but the variations in health plans. The regulations are constantly changing, so your doctor needs a team to assist with billing. Sometimes this is even one great office administrator. Staff work together to research requirements and adjust your health treatment plan as necessary to stay within your benefits.

However, it is a leap to think your doctor knows this off memory. The doctor or staff still needs to call the health plan to verify benefits, prior to your visit. In addition, follow-up after the visit to ensure any additional services will be in network. It's a lot of work to continuously engage with health plans.

Luckily, the internet helps slightly. Your doctor's office utilizes a provider portal, just like your member portal, for physicians. The portal allows for some verification to be done online. The majority of time your physician doesn't verify specialists are in network at the time they provide you with a referral.

If you doctor refers you to a specialist, nutritionist, radiologist, or any other physician, you should check that they are participating providers with your specific health plan. Furthermore, if you are referred to a facility, meaning laboratory, outpatient surgery center, home health, or any other institution, check to ensure that they participate with your specific health plan too.

For every medical service you receive there are two bills sent to the health plan. The first is for the physician's time and expertise and the other is for the place of service, where the visit was rendered. Therefore, **both** the physician and the facility have to be in network with your health plan.

Here is another good tip. If you are having surgery, ask if your anesthesiologist is in network. If not, expect to pay hundreds.

Your doctor hasn't memorized your health plan's network. This shifts the responsibility to you to verify treatments and providers before undergoing services. If you have an HMO or a PPO, this is important. Literally, this determines your potential payment later. If you take the time to authenticate before service, you will owe less in the end. An easy way to validate is to call the Member Services department, they can even estimate the cost for you.

The administrative side of healthcare is extremely complex. There are no guarantees. This is the reason you cannot assume your doctor knows the particulars of your health plan. It is really your obligation to follow through with your member services department. There is another burden that falls to you too.

3. <u>Get an authorization</u>

Usually, your physician will obtain the authorization for services. This is part of their or their office staff's job. The physician or office staff verifies that services are covered by contacting the health plan's provider services department prior to completing any procedures. If the service requires authorization, it must be approved by the health plan first. The health plan does have the right to deny the request. Services that are medically necessary often do not have issues being approved, but this is up to your health plan.

If an authorization is not obtained there could be consequences. There are a few different scenarios that may or may not be in your favor.

You need to obtain an authorization to see an out-of-network provider, usually if you have an HMO or want to pay lower costs. The repercussions are costly. You could end up paying for the entire visit or a large portion yourself.

Another situation that could happen is your doctor does not obtain authorization before the service is provided. In this scenario, you will find out after you receive the eligibility of benefits statement or a bill from the physician, noting a considerable patient responsibility. There is good news. Just like your health plan that is accountable for their mistakes, so is your physician. A physician cannot charge you for services, if they failed to obtain authorizations, as long as you utilize an in-network provider. The physician has to write-off the portion of the difference between their total charges and the insurance companies payment. In order to avoid these costs, you have to read your eligibility of statements from the health plan very carefully. Health plans code claims with explanations. Once you have the explanation, you can research how to resolve or call the Member Services department to find out from the claims team.

4. <u>**Sign up for your online portal**</u>

Nowadays, every provider that you go to asks you to sign up or offers a patient portal. There are so many it is hard to keep track. A patient portal is a web-based software program that stores all your healthcare information. Most often let you communicate directly with your provider or health plan directly. There are great advantages to signing up. However, selecting the best option is tough.

Definitely, sign up for your health plan's patient portal. This gives you access to all your information in one area. There is a section for benefits with detailed information by service as well as a provider directory that notes the difference in cost by provider. If you are lucky, there is also a cost estimator. Usually, health plan's note cheaper options for urgent care and pharmacy choices. This points you in the right direction.

In addition, the health plan tracks all your bills (claims) from each service utilized. You have access to view eligibility of benefit statements, claims, and find material on how everything was processed. This way, you don't have to keep a cabinet pull of information. With everything in one place, this also allows easy matchup to physician bills. You can ask questions and file appeals claims quickly and electronically.

There are a variety of advantages, including wellness tips, incentives, bill pay, health challenges, etc. If you are with a health plan that is affiliated with a hospital, physician group, etc., all this data is available through the same portal too. For example, Kaiser Permanente has a health plan, but also hospitals, physicians, pharmacies, and lots of other facilities. Their portal is a fully integrated care management system.

The other good patient portals are from your primary care provider and ob-gyn. You do not need to sign up for each patient portal available or offered, just the most utilized ones.

Where to Start Recap

It is not easy to interpret the language of healthcare, especially when most information is coded. Healthcare professionals write for each other, not a general audience. This makes it extremely frustrating for you to navigate and coordinate administratively. However, there are a few basics to keep in mind to help keep you in control. Each suggestion will regulate costs by eliminating errors and enhancing communication.

Insight starts with checking with your health plan beforehand. Whether or not your doctor strongly suggests services are covered. This way if an authorization is necessary, it's obtained early in the process. Following these suggestions before services are provided will eliminate problems later and/or very high bills. Additionally, signing up for your patient portal offers quick access to resources to track, manage, and control costs.

Lightning Facts

Need to Know Facts

There are really a few steps to guarantee you are paying correctly. While it may seem like a nuisance, the costs add up quickly

1. Call prior to every service, making sure to ask:

   Is my doctor in-network?
   Is this service covered under my plan?

What will be my cost for this service?
Do I need to know anything else before I
go for my visit?

2. Write down everything you are told, including who you spoke to and the date
3. Your doctor(s) have the same billing problems and often do not know if it's a covered service until their office staff call to ask.
4. Your doctor and <u>YOU</u> are required to get an authorization, so make sure you get one.
5. Your health portal tracks all your medical expenses, benefit summaries, health information, and much, more.

Take a Moment

Register for your health portal

Look up your eligibility of benefit statements on your health portal. Do these statements match the bills from your doctor? They should.

Chapter 5 – Bills, Bills, Bills

Find Errors Quickly and Efficiently

Bills, Bills, Bills

It is impossible to have complete accuracy over our healthcare claims/bills, despite our attempts for perfection. Each provider tries to bill in agreement with the guidelines and regulations, as health plans try to process claims adhering to these same principles. However, system and human error exists. Benefits and configurations change quarterly, annually, which help foster billing mistakes.

This is the reason you need to check everything. It could easily be the difference between bankruptcy and owing your deductible. Although, these days with the high deductible plan trend, even meeting your deductible means you will still owe a lot of money. The point is error exists and is common.

There are Federal and State regulations mandating payment standards. The most well-known regulation is the *Clean Claims Act*, which states that claims must be processed in a timely manner. However, the caveat is the claim has to be "clean." This means the physician must bill correctly, otherwise the health plan can reject the claim. Rejecting the claim, means the health plan renders a denial to the physician to correct the claim. The physician must correct the issue and re-submit. This process continues until the claim is considered "clean" by the health plan. Once the claim is "clean", the health plan has to process within 30 days. The only item you may receive is a notice from the health plan, in a form of an explanation of benefits. Otherwise, we are not involved in this process, until the bill arrives a little while later.

The American Medical Academy (AMA) produces a report on the major health plans. Their findings are important as they pinpoint potential sources of improvement in health plan processes. "The AMA estimates that $12 billion a year could be saved if insurers eliminated unnecessary administrative tasks with automated systems for processing and paying medical claims. This savings represents 21 percent of total administrative costs that physicians spend to ensure accurate payments from insurers (http://www.policymed.com/2013/07/amas-national-health-insurer-report-card-12-billion-could-be-saved-through-increased-claims-automation.html, 2013)."

There is good news. Health plans worked effectively in 2013 to increase accuracy. The problem is there is no way to truly understand how this was measured with 100% accuracy. Now these statistics are prior to the ACA International Statistical Classification of Diseases and Related Health Problems version10 ICD-10 implementation. Bottom line, even if claims processing is improving, you still need to regularly check your bills and explanation of benefits (EOB's). There is really only one exact method to validate.

Two-Step Verification

1. *Keep your EOB from the insurance company. Usually, the eligibility of benefits statement will be posted to your health portal or mailed to you personally.*
2. *Once the bill arrives from the physician, hospital, or other type of provider, compare the statements. Even though both are written in a secret language of code, they should both match. The description of the services should help you align costs between the documents. The eligibility of benefits statement has a section for patient responsibility, which includes deductible, co-pay, and co-insurance. These amounts should be identical to the bill from the physician that denotes your total amount owed. If there are any differences or services that appear odd, give your member services center a call. You only have a few weeks to report issues, so the sooner the better.*

Health plans will assist if you point out an issue, but rarely does the organization go looking for problems.

It is up to you to find and report them. In order to have your health plan address your issue, you need to report it within a specific time. Generally, you have anywhere between 90-180 days to submit appeals. Appeals have to be in writing in the exact format denoted to you in your benefits booklet/EOP from the health plan. If the proper format is not followed, the health plan will not review the document. Also, you have 1 – 2 changes before you exhaust your appeal rights. Basically, you have one shot at getting the health plan to correct before you are out of options.

Health plans count on the appeal process being too excessive for most people and therefore the volume of member appeals will be low. This thought process is often very accurate. However, you have better than a 50/50 chance of your claim being reprocessed for more money through the appeals process. The other major point is benefit issues can also be submitted for an appeal, not just claim issues. Benefit issues are what services are included in your plan being applied correctly when your claims are processed.

Once appeal rights are exhausted, there are still available options for you. If you have insurance through your employer, contact your HR office as they may be able to help. If you are independent or cannot obtain resolution from any other avenue, write to your state insurance administration. Again, there is a specific format and time limit, which is denoted on the applicable state website. Usually, you will need to fill out a form and attach all your correspondence and supporting documentation associated with the issue.

The trick is to use keywords in your write-up. You have to write for the audience, so in these cases, we mean technical healthcare jargon. Consult an expert, such as Healthcare Deciphered prior to submitting the paperwork. Also, an "authorized user" can submit appeals on your behalf. This is important as it may very well be worth the money, time, and frustration to pay for these services. Just be careful if a company wants a percentage of your savings. It should be a small fee, not an overall percentage.

Bills, Bills, Bills Recap

The best process to ensure you don't overpay is to appeal everything. While this may take considerable time, it is often beneficial for you. If you submit 2 appeals, 50% will likely be adjusted. That's a 1 out of 2 chance for savings. If the appeals are claims are office visits, you may save a few dollars. However, if you have hospital bills the appeals could result in much more money back for you. If you do have a high number of medical bills, calculate your out-of-pocket maximum. Once you hit this number, your responsibility ceases

Medical bills, benefit determinations, etc. is a lot to track. That's exactly what the healthcare industry is expecting. They are banking on the probability that you will lose track of your appeals or not consider appealing to be worth the hassle. However, you can always find a service to help. This service is included in the standard package from Healthcare Deciphered. If you utilize another company, just make sure you pay a flat rate as opposed to a percentage of your savings. It doesn't make sense to pay with money you should have never spent initially. Find a company that will write, submit, track, and report on the progress of your appeal.

It's definitely worth the savings, if you have a family who regularly visits the doctor. If you are pregnant or just had a baby, medical expenses add up quickly. It's always a good idea to double check. Save documentation from both the health plan and physicians. Every month set aside time to verify documents match accordingly. It's a far better option, then over spending.

Lightning Facts

Need to Know Facts

Accuracy is a two-step verification process. Employ this process each time you receive a bill from the doctor. The health plan sends their information about the bill prior to you receiving the doctor's bill. Therefore, you have everything to check.

1. Verify differences in your eligibility of benefits statement and doctor's bill prior to contacting the health plan.
2. You have a 50% chance your claim will be re-processed, so try!
3. Still have questions? Contact our team to help you ensure accuracy: customerservice@healthcaredeciphered.com

Take a Moment

Since you've started to verify costs, are you wondering what the average costs are for services? There are plenty of sources online now to help. Here are a few to get you started:

Medical

Healthcare Bluebook: http://fairhealth
consumer.org/medicalcostlookup.php

Fair Health Consumer: http://fairhealth
consumer.org/medicalcostlookup.php

Truven Health: http://truvenhealth.com/
solutions/treatment-cost-calculator

Pharmacy

Pharmacy Quote: https://www.rxpricequotes.
com/

Good Rx: http://www.goodrx.com/

PS – Your Health Portal should have one too!

Chapter 6 – Get Resolution

A Guide to Getting Results

Get Resolution

There are different options you can take to get a favorable resolution from your health plan. The variance is determined by the path taken and words spoken. Key words are the hidden gem to obtaining a fast resolution. However, learning the language to speak is the most difficult part. There are a few terms, specialized to the health care industry, with which everyone should be familiar. These are not ordinarily defined or used words except for within health care.

Reconsideration

This process is very similar to the appeals process, but without the paperwork. Most people have to call their health plan to inquire about benefits, claims (bills), authorizations, etc. We've previously discussed you are calling the Member Services department, who serve as the gatekeepers to other departments. If the Member Services representative confirms there is a problem with a benefit or claim while on the phone, you will be directed to file a formal appeal. However, there is another way. Ask for a reconsideration instead. Reconsideration is an expedited process, where a Member Services representative sends your case back to the processing area to re-review. If the team determines an error occurred, usually the health plan will fix the issue. This process typically takes about 10 business days, but varies by health plan. The caveat is this is not applicable to traditional Medicare/Medicaid plans, unless your health plan is provided by another organization.

A Member Services representative will call you back after the reconsideration request has been reviewed. If you do not obtain your desired resolution, you will have to submit a formal appeal. However, if your decision is overturned, you should receive an updated letter, EOB, or other document from the health plan denoting the change. If you are successful, this is all you need to do to get a favorable resolution.

Complaint

A complaint is defined as a statement regarding a situation that was unsatisfactory or unacceptable (quote). In healthcare, complaints are common, also known as grievances. Thousands of grievances are submit per plan per year However, there would probably be grievances filed more if this option was better known and described to members of the health plan. There are often times a health plan or provider provides subpar care or service. The good news is there is an organization that is tracking, following up, and reporting on complaints. Your health plan is regulated by law to follow-up on the validity of any complaint it receives. Complaints could be regarding waiting too long to see your doctor, someone saying something inappropriate or inaccurate, being told services could not be provided, etc. In addition, if you receive inadequate care, this to can be reported to your health plan. You can even file a complaint with your health plan about the health plan, if needed. Every complaint must be investigated and responded to within 30 days. This is standard practice within the health care industry.

Whether or not your issue is resolved within 30 days depends on the regulations in your state. However, you can rest assured that the case has been looked into by this time. Health plans take complaints very seriously, no matter to whom the complaint pertains.

To file a complaint, you will have to write to the health plan. However, a letter describing the problem will generally suffice. Sometimes there is a form to fill out; both are mailed to the health plan for review. This is generally a less formal process as opposed to filing an appeal.

This is a quick tip, Consumer Reports or the Better Business Bureau track complaints about health plans. Healthcare companies are businesses, so these organizations are monitored alongside every other industry. Health Grades reports on provider's complaints and status. In addition, any of the federal or state health care agencies offer instructions on their websites about how to file a complaint. These are helpful tools to review prior to selecting a health plan or provider. On most of these types of websites, you can even write a review.

The good news about complaints is you don't need key words to get resolution. Simply state the problem and the reason for filing the complaint.

Appeals

The appeals process is more commonly known, as it is at least advertised by health plans and doctors. Doctors also submit appeals, just like you. The process can be long and challenging. The best advice is to get into the practice of appealing your claims on a regular basis, especially if you visit multiple doctors or facilities. There is a 50/50 chance the appealed decision will be in your favor. It also is a way to ensure you don't overpay for services, as a different department reviews all the appeals. The claims department reviews the claims initially and/

or the system processes the claims automatically. Automatically means the claim is paid based on the system configuration as updated at the time of your claim. No one personally reviews the claim, unless it is a high dollar amount. Most claims are reviewed over a certain amount, for example $10K. This is to ensure high dollar claims are not paid erroneously. However, during the appeals process, representatives from the Appeals department and clinical staff, review your claim. Therefore, it is to your advantage, as fresh eyes review your case.

The appeals process is actually the best way to get money back that you never should have paid initially. As we've discussed earlier, there is a specific way to write up the appeal to submit to the health plan. If your letter does not include these criteria, it will not be considered. This is important as you have one right to appeal. Afterwards, you will have to escalate to human resources, state insurance commission, or take other legal action.

There are ways to find the appeal criteria easily. The 1st place is on the bottom of the EOB in fine print. The information will include the criteria necessary to submit a "qualifying" appeal, submission address, and overall process. The 2nd place is on the health plan's website, which should have multiple links to the appeals instructions. This criterion is listed in your portal, usually an option on the same screen as the claim or electronic EOB information. The health plan also publishes the appeals process on the member and provider homepages. If you still cannot locate the appeals process, there should be a search function of the health plan's website too. Use the term "appeal" to search the health plan's website. There may be a few options in the search result, but one will be the information you need to submit an appeal appropriately. The last option is to call Member Services to request the Appeals process verbally over the phone. This is not an option utilized much, as the information is available online.

Conclusion

The best way to obtain a favorable resolution is to utilize the resources that you now know are available to you. The overarching problem is determining whether or not there is an issue. Therefore, the best advice is to appeal everything that seems even a little bit off. Again, there is a 50/50 chance that your claim will be overturned on re-evaluation by the health plan. Before you pay a few hundred dollars or more use the reconsideration, complaint, or appeals process. Even if you do not receive any refunds, you've at least verified the claim paid correctly. This approach assures you that the process is working correctly. Cost verification in the healthcare industry is extremely difficult to validate. Members pay 25% of the overall cost of healthcare out-of-pocket and $1.5 billion of this cost is due to inaccurate claim payments. Don't leave money on the table if you can avoid it.

Lightning Facts

Need to Know Facts

It's good to know you still have options, even after you may have lost hope. There are always possibilities.

1. Resolution options for your health plan are provided in several places:

   Eligibility of Benefit Statements
   Health Plan website.... You guessed it, also on your health portal site!

2. Follow the guidelines exactly as outlined by your health plan to submit complaints or appeals
3. The health plan must respond to your concern within 30 days.

Take a Moment

Have you used one of these options? If not, login to your health portal to review the process. Print out the instructions for each process and keep with your medical records. This way you have the instructions available to you, when you need to utilize. It's important to be prepared.

Chapter 7 – What's Next?

Get to a Better Health care State

Get to a Better State of Health Care

The goal of the guidance found in this book is to provide assurance that is difficult to find in the health care field. It is my hope that by offering an array of tips directly from the health care experts that you will be able to get to a better state of health care. This information is practical for businesses, families, and individuals who have any type of health insurance. Health plans offer a variety of different plans but the core operations are relatively similar for each company. This is beneficial, as the information above is universal. While the health plan fine print all differs, the types of services offered are also fairly similar.

Benefits change at least annually, so it is important to compare the types of services each year in your plan to foreshadow cost changes. Even if you keep the same plan year over year it is likely there are some differences. Health plans are required to alert you every year of the plan updates. Usually, you will receive a letter in the mail describing the changes in detail or at least an overview. It is up to you at this point to estimate the impact. To help anticipate the highest impact, quickly check there are no significant changes to the top 5 services you utilize throughout the year. If you are anticipating a surgery, double check the costs before you re-elect. The surgery itself may not be covered, the codes covered by health plans change regularly. Therefore, a surgery covered one year may not be covered the subsequent year. This is in additional to benefit or service changes to the plan. Anticipating the financial effect of major health care decisions will help to eliminate surprises throughout the year. Now there are a few tricks to remember your benefits.

Easily Remember your Benefits

At the doctor's office, have you been asked about the amount of your copay? Or has the receptionist questioned what is covered under your plan? There are a multitude of medical plans nationally, so it is difficult for the doctor's office to recall all the intricate details of each health care plan. With all the different terminology, it is even challenging for us to remember all our own benefits. However, there are a few simple ways to have your benefits accessible to you at any time.

TIP 1

Most insurance companies have mobile apps now, particularly the larger carriers. You can download the app from the insurance company's website quickly. It will not be on your phone's online store. The catch is you have to be registered on the company's main website before you can use the mobile app. Registering with your health plan's health portal is beneficial to you. Once registered and using the the mobile app, you will be able to lookup participating physicians and identify urgent care locations as well. You can also easily reference your coverage, benefits, and copies of your member ID while using the app as well.

TIP 2

If you do not have wireless service or if your insurance company does not offer a mobile app, there are a few other ways to access your medical information easily. Most cell phones have picture capability, which you can use to your benefit. During the annual enrollment period and every year afterwards, insurance plans send out Summary of Coverage documents. I've included an example below of a Summary of Coverage document. Once you receive the summary, take a picture of each of the pages. This way you can easily forward benefit details to physicians or reference when questions arise. The information will be stored as a picture on your phone until you choose to delete it.

TIP 3

There is also the option of adding a note to your phone. This is a more manual approach, but completely worth the time to enter the information. You really only need to note a few items, such as member ID, deductible, provider network phone line, referral requirements, medical copay, pharmacy copay, outpatient surgery copay, hospital admission copay, co-insurance %, and what's not covered. Listing the services that are not covered is essential. If you need a service that is not covered under your plan, find out the total cost of the service a head of time, as you may have to pay the full cost in the end. You can work through this issue with your health plan, but always be prepared as providers will bill you for services if the insurance company does not cover the service.

TIP 4

The last option is to keep your Summary of Coverage or a quick reference guide in your wallet. This information can be folded to fit in a slot for a credit card or kept in the same area where you store your bills. While it might seem odd to carry this information in your wallet since you don't need regularly, you will find it helpful to have the information accessible when you need it. When the moment arises that you need your benefits, which usually happens in emergencies, you don't want additional stress trying to research your benefits. If you keep the information close, there will be little chance of confusion for your physician in regards to your benefits because you have all your benefits ready in hand.

If you only have time to take away one tip for remembering your medical benefits, my last suggestion is to memorize or store the member benefit number. This information is usually listed on the back of your insurance card. You can always store as an image on your phone. If there is any doubt, it's better to call your insurance company to check. A quick conversation should clarify any questions or concerns about services. Remembering your benefits is an easy way to help your providers limit confusion or billing errors.

Conclusion

The combination above allows you to get to a better health care state. There are creative ways to cut medical costs if you are able to navigate healthcare efficiently. Start with accessing a more knowledgeable health care team. It is always better to ask questions and track the conversations, but you have to take it a step further. Make sure you ask the experts. Remember, this is accomplished by requesting that certain departments handle your claim(s) directly and/or speaking in health care terminology. The better versed you are in the process the easier it will be to get accurate information from your health plan. This helps you start out on the right path to a better health care state. While it seems counter-intuitive, your doctor is not always the best source to help with administrative support as his or her background is clinical. Odds are your doctor(s) struggle with the same issues as you do. While this is likely accidental, errors exist throughout the billing process from providers to health plans.

Make sure to cross-reference your EOB's with bills from the doctor to validate costs. This is the fastest, easiest, and most efficient method to find errors. If you find something that seems strange, speak up. You are on a time clock. If your time expires, you will be stuck with the consequences, which usually equal a payment from you. While it is a little tedious to call or write your health plan, the advantages outweigh the lengthy time process. Again, there is a 50/50 chance your claim will be re-processed in your favor on appeal. Get in the habit of asking for reconsiderations or writing formal appeals. You will have a rhythm after a couple of times of writing appeals. The cost advantages outweigh the time required to submit for resolution. If you appeal online through your health plan's portal, it is also generally a little faster.

We focus on the administrative process, but there are a variety of medical cost-saving tips available. Online at www.blog.healthcaredeciphered.com, there are steps for savings on medical debt, prescription costs, and a number of other articles to limit the financial impact of healthcare. There is also a variety of sites that provide information, just use the key words in your search. As a community, we have to put our resources together to effect change in the health care processes.

Healthcare Deciphered Handbook

Healthcare is a confusing and frustrating industry with lots of guidelines, mostly unknown to you. In order to help we've provided a quick reference Handbook. It is simple to get clarity when you have the right tools.

1. The average family spends $25,000 a year on healthcare (including premiums, deductibles, co-insurance, and other out of pocket expenses)
2. Costs are increasing overall for physicians and insurance companies, which are being pushed to you
3. Contributing to a large portion of the overall costs are errors
4. The majority of people do not have any idea how to check for accuracy

5. Health plans are similar, so one set of guidelines can be applied universally to get cost verification for you.

6. Member Services department is your primary source for health benefit, network, and claim questions.

7. Member services acts as a call center and is staffed by people who likely do not have a healthcare degree of any kind.

8. Sales Agents and Brokers setup your health coverage. Once active, member services staff is responsible for helping with any additional questions.

9. Your employer's Human Resources department is the best option for enrollment, problem resolution, and any other questions you may have on your employer-based insurance.

10. However, the Human Resources staff often do not have a background in health plan operations and this may limit the degree of assistance you receive from your office's HR department.

11. Doctors struggle with the same issues you face. There are too many different health plans and products to easily master the process and requirement for each.

12. Utilization and Case Managers are certified nurses and clinical staff with medical training. This area can help explain:

> Authorization requirements
> Approved health plan services
> Help m*anage your health*

13. Network Specialists are the best resource to help identify doctors, facilities, and hospitals you can utilize. They can also help approve exceptions if there is a service gap.

14. Claim Specialists have intimate knowledge about how claims are processed. If anyone can help you verify accuracy, they certainly can review.

15. Appeals and Grievances are the last option to get resolution. We saved the best for last.

16. Make sure to get transferred appropriately to the right area.

17. Use these resources to get absolute clarity

18. Call prior to every service, making sure to ask:

> *Is my doctor in-network?*
> *Is this service covered under my plan?*
> *What will be my cost for this service?*
> *Do I need to know anything else before I go for my visit?*

19. Write down everything you are told, including who you spoke to and the date of the conversation

20. Your doctor(s) have the same billing problems and often do not know if it's a covered service until their office staff call to ask.

21. Your doctor and <u>YOU</u> are required to get an authorization, so make sure you get one.

22. Your health portal tracks all your medical expenses, benefit summaries, health information, and much, much, more

23. You have a 50% chance your claim will be re-processed, so try!

24. Verify differences in your eligibility of benefits statement and doctor's bill prior to contacting the health plan.

25. Still have questions? Contact our team to help you ensure accuracy: <u>customerservice@healthcaredeciphered. com</u>

26. Resolution options for your health plan are provided in several places:

Eligibility of Benefit Statements
Health Plan website.... You guessed it, also on your health portal site!

27. Follow the guidelines exactly as outlined by your health plan to submit complaints or appeals
28. The health plan must respond to your concern within 30 days.

Printed in the United States
By Bookmasters